The BBC reports . . .

This booklet gives a brief account of the BBC's work in television, radio and world broadcasting. It is based mainly on the Annual Report and Accounts for 1975–6 which the Board of Governors presents to the Home Secretary and to Parliament. The full story is to be found in the BBC Handbook 1977. But as this runs to 350 pages and costs £1.50 (incidentally, the same price as last year) we thought our licence-payers might like us to make a shorter version available.

Details of all programmes in RadioTimes

John Gielgud in the BBC / Open University
production of *The Brothers Karamazov*

SATURDAY NIGHT ON THE BBC
MOZART 50
VILLA 3 SPURS 1
DERBY 2 LEEDS
MAN.U 1 WBA 1
QPR 2 ARSENAL
POOLS
BBC 2
Larry

Fact: In 1975 – 6 a total of 11,259 hours of television programmes was transmitted by the BBC. The average viewer watched over nine hours a week.

Fact: During the same year BBC Radio broadcast 116,555 hours of programmes. The average listener heard over eight hours a week.

The choice can be bewildering . . . .

Scene: 2 October 1976, the suburban home of a not-too-typical family (with *two* TV sets!).

5.10 pm The kids have just finished watching *Tom and Jerry* on BBC 1. Mum and Dad join them for the *News.*

5.25 *The Wonderful World of Disney.* Mum stays for 45 minutes before putting the dinner on. Dad's gone to double-check his pools coupon on Radio 2's *Sports Report.* His eldest boy, John, likes news of the local match on the BBC Local Radio station.

5.31 Teen-ager Suzie's upstairs in her bedroom, catching *It's Rock 'n' Roll* on Radio 1, followed by *In Concert,* both in stereo.

6.10 Time for *Dr. Who* on BBC 1. A new four-part story, *The Hand of Fear.* Dad's back again (he's as much of a fan as the kids, but he won't let on).

6.15 On his portable, John's watching *Network,* one of BBC 2's half-hour offerings from the regions. Called *The Man who sells Jesus,* it's about an evangelist who fills his Bristol church with youngsters every Sunday night.

6.35 *Bruce Forsyth and The Generation Game.* Mum says it's daft really, but the family do come trickling in to watch. They say he gets over 20 million watching sometimes.

7.25 *The Duchess of Duke Street.* It's only been on five weeks and some people are already planning their evenings so they don't miss it. Ten million on the first night, 13 million the following week. Dad says he fancies the quail pudding. Mum says he'll be lucky.

8.15 *The Two Ronnies.* Dad's still chuckling over the one the other week about crossing the elephant with the Axminster carpet. He and Mum agreed to watch it on the portable, so that John and Suzie could watch BBC 2's *The Lively Arts – In Performance* on the colour set. They've got *The Barber of Seville* from La Scala, Milan, and it's even better if you listen to Radio 3's simultaneous broadcast in stereo.

8.30 Mum's gone to the kitchen to do the washing-up. To tell the truth, she wants to catch Radio 4's *Saturday Night Theatre,* too, followed by the 10 o'clock *News.*

9.00 Now Suzie's got a problem. You can't watch opera and *Starsky & Hutch* at the same time. The newspapers are full of it – and so are the girls at school. Dad says it's time for the kids to go to bed (loud protests) because of what he's read about it in *Radio Times.* Then he settles down to watch this week's episode, 'Las Vegas Strangler'.

10.30 Mum's off to bed with her transistor for *A Word in Edgeways.* Dad likes the way Angela Rippon brings him the *News* and the weather.

10.40 Dad's staying up for *Match of the Day* (John will be in shortly, after the opera).

11.40 Suzie joins them for *Parkinson* (guest this week: Sammy Davis, Jnr.), after watching another Bristol programme on BBC 2, *The Gamekeeper,* a documentary about the annual cycle of life on a Wessex farm. Mum says they'll all get square eyes. Dad wonders what you get, in that case, if you're still listening to Radio 2's *The Late Show* in bed at midnight when she's supposed to be having an early night.

● The family's £18 colour TV licence meant the *whole day's* services cost them less than 5p (an £8 black-and-white licence gives you a day's broadcasting for a little over 2p).

(P.S. every TV *and radio set has an* OFF *switch too)*

Richard Vernon and Gemma Jones in *The Duchess of Duke Street*

To the news staff at Bush House one recent letter stood out because it was from a fellow professional of some distinction. Malcolm W. Browne, Eastern Europe correspondent of the *New York Times*, wrote in the course of a letter:

'I can only say that the BBC serves not only as a beacon to ordinary listeners, but as a standard against which all news correspondents of the free world compare their own work.

'During much of my own career I have been entirely cut off from other sources of information – in Vietnam, Pakistan, the hinterlands of South America, the Spanish Sahara and so forth – but for the BBC. It has enabled me to maintain a perspective without which my own reporting would have suffered.

'It seems unfair that the British Government and people alone should have to bear the cost of this matchless enterprise, but there is obviously no alternative. One can only hope that Britain will sustain the will to go on with the BBC more or less as it is. BBC is, for the free mind, what Oxfam is for the hungry.'

Bush House is between Fleet Street and Trafalgar Square. It's the headquarters of the BBC External Services. They broadcast to the world in English and 38 other languages. Funds are voted annually by Parliament, instead of coming out of the licence money.

Bush is on the air, round the globe, for 704 hours a week. This is how they spent some of those hours on the evening of Saturday, 2 October, 1976.

5.00 pm The Hindi Service. Listeners in Delhi (where it's 9.30 pm) can hear a bulletin of world news, an international sports round-up and a 15-minute week-end review including an item on the women's peace movement in Northern Ireland.

6.15 The World Service is broadcasting *This Week and Africa*, an English language programme specially prepared for African listeners. In East Africa, for instance, it's 8.15 pm when you hear 30 minutes of background to the week's major news stories. And it's been a busy week, including negotiations on Rhodesia, speculation about President Kenyatta's successor and the resumption of diplomatic relations between Angola and Portugal.

8.00 It's two hours later in Moscow, where you can hear the Russian Service with a world news summary and *Saturday Pops*. One of the Service's producers remembers fondly listening to pop and jazz on the BBC when he was in his home town of Leningrad four years ago.

9.15 The World Service's International Press Review is going out. Devoted to round-the-world newspaper coverage of Dr. Kissinger's shuttle diplomacy, it's the only source of such news in many countries.

10.00 German Service news bulletin – including latest news of the International Monetary Fund's reaction to Britain's application for a loan.

11.30 Breakfast-time on Sunday morning in Peking, as the Chinese Service bring a world news bulletin to another country.

**The Last Night of the Proms
is the culmination of a two-month music festival,
organised and financed by the BBC.
As well as the domestic broadcasting coverage –
with all Proms live on Radio 3 and several on Television –
many are also transmitted on the BBC World Service.**

Inflation hits everybody . . .
even Captain Mainwaring is in the same boat.
At the start of *Dad's Army* in 1968,
an episode cost slightly less than £9,000.
When the last series was made in 1975
an episode should have cost almost £20,000
with the inflation of the last seven years.
(Captain Mainwaring, as a good bank manager,
kept the cost down to just over £18,000.)

No one could call the platoon's accommodation luxurious –
the same draughty church hall and office leading off it
they've used from the beginning; and the same
modest office from which Captain Mainwaring manages the bank.
The only difference is that it now costs the BBC
twice as much to build them.

As the BBC's Board of Governors says in the first sentence of its annual report to Parliament: 'We must begin with **inflation**'.

Doesn't everything these days? But inflation hits the BBC budget just as much as it hits the household budget.

It's a menace

● to *development*, like building more TV transmitters;

● to *programmes*, forcing still more reductions;

● to our *financial strategy*, the plan to live within our means after licences last went up in April, 1975.

We'd made some cuts then. Like the Government, we wanted to make sure licences didn't need to go up again for at least two years. And it seemed we could reach the end of March, 1977, with any deficit kept within acceptable limits.

All the savings targets set then were reached. Even exceeded.

But the financial climate was getting worse.

Inflation was making it more difficult for viewers to rent or buy colour TV. That meant less money than we or the Government had expected from colour licences.

On top of that, our costs went up still further. For instance, to cover its own mounting expenses, the Post Office put up its charges for collecting the licence fee in the first place.

What was left was buying less and less.

The prospect was depressing. And, for the BBC, it wasn't a familiar one. It's only in recent years that we've had to borrow at all – even after more than half a century's broadcasting.

And we'd never before even considered the possibility of borrowing everything we could raise.

A substantial deficit puts the BBC's independence at risk. And the high cost of borrowing diverts money which would otherwise be spent on programmes.

But the alternatives would have included swingeing cuts in programmes – bad for the audience, bad for the employment of writers, artists and staff.

Even now, we've had to make extra cuts amounting to £10 million. That's why there have been more repeats on television than we'd all prefer (although some, like *Dad's Army*, are very popular). Programme budgets have been tightened, too.

If you haven't noticed, it's thanks to the ingenuity of the programme-makers.

Administrative costs have been pruned, too, right across the board.

Despite everything, then, our prices – the licences for black-and-white and colour television – will have been pegged for two years (which is more than a lot of people can say).

Without inflation, we wouldn't need to ask for licences to go up at all in 1977.

In what the economists call 'real terms' – leaving aside the effects of inflation – **the cost of the BBC's services has been falling regularly in recent years,** *because we use our resources efficiently.*

Imagine there wasn't any inflation. Then the money we'd get for extra colour licences would have meant

no increase for about ten years.

It may be small comfort when you're struggling with inflation yourself.

But, at least, it may put things into perspective.

Madame Bovary: Francesca Annis, Tom Conti and Denis Lill

The Liver Birds: Nerys Hughes and Elizabeth Estensen (top left); *Fawlty Towers:* Connie Booth and John Cleese (top right); *I Didn't Know You Cared* (above); and Shirley Bassey (left)

This is what a television licence would cost you in these European countries. **Grey** shows the fee for a monochrome licence,
and **Green** the fee for colour
. . . and only BBC, Denmark and Sweden **do not have advertising income** as well.

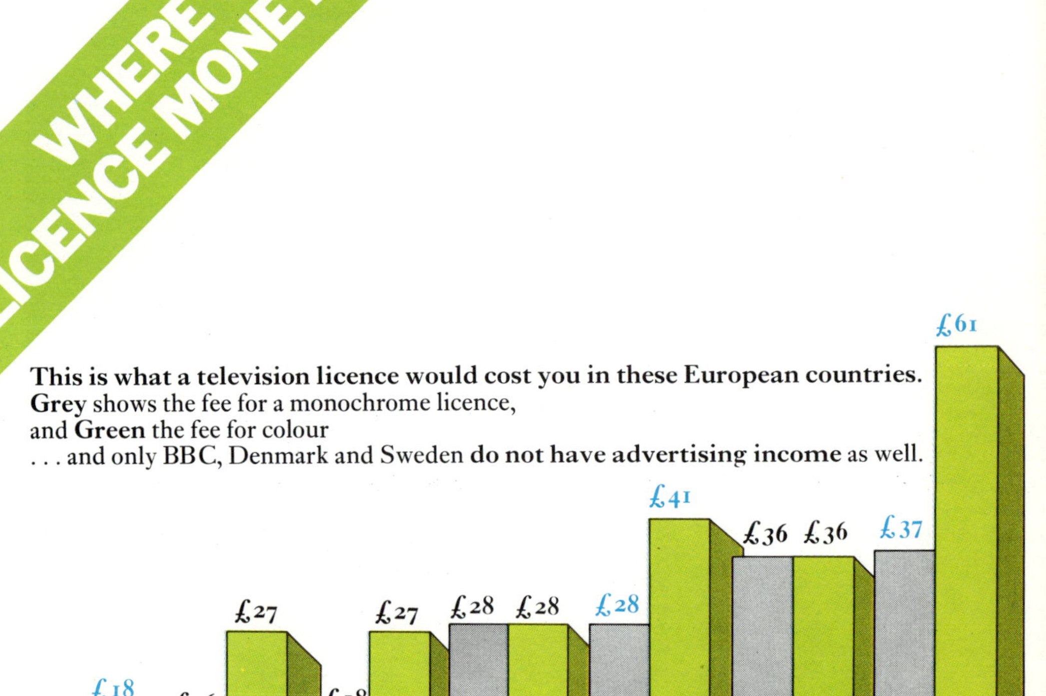

Licence fees in European countries

If you were on holiday in Europe last summer, you will know that most things there are more expensive than in Britain. But even so, the difference in what it costs to view television is fairly striking. Our licence fee costs far less than in any other European country. We often pay less than half what they do for colour, and less than a quarter for monochrome.

Here are a few countries – with figures given to us by the European Broadcasting Union last July, when the pound was worth more in European currencies than it is today.

Money in 1975–6

Nearly half the licence payers in the country had colour sets and bought an £18 licence.
The rest paid £8 for their black & white licence.

£ million

This amounted to	234
and after paying the Post Office for collecting licences, dealing with evaders and interference investigation	21
the BBC was left with	213
Profits after tax of came from *Radio Times,* the sale of TV programmes, gramophone records & other commercial activities	2
so at the beginning of the year it was	215
but the BBC was 'in the red' by	19
which left us with	196

in 1975–76 to pay for

- two national colour television channels
- regional television services
- four network radio services
- regional radio services
- twenty local radio stations

Money out 1975–6

Television cost	132
and Radio cost	52
and a further was spent on renewing equipment, providing new transmitters and improving production facilities particularly in the Regions	18
	202
which means that at the end of the year the BBC was still 'in the red', but the amount had been reduced to	6

(See also pages 46–7)

Two new Further Education series:
(top) *Dressmaker*, for which these
special clothes were designed;
and *Mr Smith's Flower Garden*

How Green Was My Valley (top),
and Jessica Benton in *The Onedin Line*

The largest BBC *television audiences* of the year were recorded on Christmas Day, 1975, with *Morecambe and Wise* and *Some Mothers Do 'ave 'em* topping 25 million.

The annual Miss World and Eurovision Song Contests came close behind with about 24 million.

Of the regular series, the biggest attractions were *The Generation Game* and *The Two Ronnies*, both of which were seen each week by about 18 million viewers. Many other light entertainment series drew between 12 and 15 million.

Similar sized audiences were attracted by the American imports *Kojak* and *The Invisible Man* (14 million), by the short season of Carry On films (13 million) and by the drama series *When The Boat Comes In* (12.5 million).

Other noteworthy drama series were *The Brothers* (11 million) and *Poldark* (almost nine million). New plays broadcast in Play for Today were seen by an average audience of six million.

Documentary series on BBC 1 averaged about five million and the three entitled *The Changing Face of Medicine* were particularly well-received by viewers.

BBC 1's main News at 9.00 pm had audiences averaging a little under eight million, as did *Nationwide* earlier in the evening. Panorama was seen each week by about four million.

It's a Knockout still headed the audiences for outside events, being seen each week by almost 14 million viewers. *Superstars* came hot on its heels at about 13 million. *Match of the Day* followed with 10.5 million, while *Sportsnight* had an average audience of nine million.

Among children's programmes the ever popular series *Dr.Who* had audiences of 10 million. *Basil Brush* eight million, *Crackerjack* 6.5 million and *Blue Peter* some five million. The quiz *Top of the Form* was seen on average by 13.5 million viewers.

Some Mothers Do 'ave 'em: Michael Crawford (top); *Eurovision Song Contest*: the winners – 'Brotherhood of Man' (left); and *Bruce Forsyth and The Generation Game*: with Anthea Redfern

BBC 2 gained 10 million viewers for its showing of *The Goodies*, and *The Waltons* remained popular, being watched each week by nearly six million people. Audiences for the classics on BBC 2 were generally in the region of one to two million, a notable exception being *Moll Flanders* which had an audience approaching six million.

The most popular radio series of the year was *Tom Browne's Top Twenty*, gaining an average audience of just under seven million, followed by *Junior Choice* with 5.5 million on Saturdays and just over four million on Sundays. The audience for Family Favourites remained stable at about 4.5 million. Among other regular programmes *Jimmy Savile* had an audience of 2.5 million, *Your Hundred Best Tunes* and *Woman's Hour* 800,000, *Gardeners' Question Time* 750,000, *Beat the Record* 500,000, *Jack de Manio Precisely, Three in a Row* 450,000, and *Motoring and the Motorist* 400,000.

The 8.00 am news on Radio 4 is listened to by just over three million people, while the section of *Today* which immediately follows this bulletin still commands an audience of two million. Both the 1.00 pm *News Bulletin* on Radio 4 and *Newsbeat* on Radio 1 have audiences of two million (the later edition of *Newsbeat* has 350,000 listeners). *PM* has an audience of 700,000.

When The Boat Comes In (top): John Nightingale, Michele Newell, Susan Jameson and James Bolam; Telly Savalas *Kojak*; and *Poldark*: Robin Ellis and Angharad Rees.

William Hardcastle (photographed here with his former editor, Andrew Boyle) died in November, 1975 – seven months after the Radio Industries Club had chosen *The World at One* as Programme of the Year

November, 1975, marked a notable scoop for BBC Television – both the International Emmy Awards.

The International Council of the National Academy of Television Arts and Sciences announced in New York that the award for non-fiction programmes had been won by *Marek*, the story of a seven year-old boy undergoing a hole-in-the-heart operation, and that the winner of the award for fiction or entertainment programmes was *The Evacuees*, Jack Rosenthal's semi-autobiographical story of two small Jewish boys who were evacuated from their home during World War II and given shelter by a gentile couple in Blackpool.

Marek was shown in the *Inside Story* series on BBC 2 in May 1975. Originally, producer Roger Mills had intended to cover the whole process of Marek's operation through to the point of recuperation. Tragically Marek died shortly after the operation, but the boy's parents felt that the film should still be shown. It was directed by Mark Anderson and has also won the Asian Broadcasting Union Prize.

The Evacuees was first shown on BBC 2 in March 1975 and was produced by Mark Shivas and directed by Alan Parker.

The BBC also won a 1975 National Emmy Award – *Profile in Music: Beverly Sills* in the classical music category. In 1976 another American Emmy was awarded to Rosemary Harris for her portrayal of George Sand in the BBC Television production *Notorious Woman*.

BBC Television won both the Drama and Documentary category awards in the Prix Italia – for *Just Another Saturday* and *Joey* respectively.

During the period 1975–6, these were among over 60 awards made to programmes, performers, writers, producers, directors, designers, cameramen, sound recordists and engineers.

BBC Radio won 20 awards during the year.

Radio 4's *The World at One* won the Radio Industries Club award for the Programme of the Year.

Radio 2's Pete Murray won the award for the Radio Personality of the Year.

The Variety Club of Britain chose David Jacobs as their Radio Personality of the Year.

The Music Trade Association award for the best speech record: *T.S.Eliot read by Alec Guinness* (originally broadcast on Radio 3)

At the UNDA International Festival of Religious Broadcasting, awards were won by the *People's Service* and by BBC Radio Manchester in the category of religious songs.

Tom Conti won the Performance Award of the Royal Television Society

Emmy winners: *The Evacuees* (top)
and Rosemary Harris in *Notorious Woman*

On the Move – the series produced as part of the BBC Adult Literacy Project –
won the Royal Television Society's 1976 Original Programme Award

'The key to the Television Service's year,' says the Annual Report, 'is the fact that it went through a period of retrenchment occasioning discomfort to itself but not to the viewer. What happened was that the amount of television broadcasting had to be reduced and money had to be made to go much further in a number of ingenious ways. But on the screen there were no signs of gloom . . .

'A principal advance during the year was in the number of good contributions to BBC 1 and BBC 2 from the three Network Production Centres in England (Bristol, Birmingham & Manchester) and from both the national and English regions.'

Music and Arts programmes prospered, with *Omnibus* including three editions in the programme's best tradition of literary biography on: Thomas Mann, John Donne and Ivy Compton-Burnett. Noteworthy music programmes included a studio production of Wagner's opera *The Flying Dutchman* and Mozart's *The Magic Flute* – broadcast simultaneously in stereo on Radio 3.

Twice during the year – in *The Fight Against Slavery* and *Explorers* – good camera direction and acting proved that an accurate documentary series can depend for its success as much on scholarly dramatic reconstructions as on the more customary studio techniques, using prints, maps and diagrams.

Three dramatic highspots of the year were the launching of special series which not only gained an immediate following of viewers but also won considerable acclaim from the critics: *Days of Hope, The Glittering Prizes* and *When the Boat Comes In.*

Right Charlie: Charlie Cairoli with young fans

It's Cliff – and Friends (top right); *Angels* (top left), Clare Clifford, Angela Bruce, Erin Geraghty, Julie Dawn Cole, Karan David and Fiona Fullerton; and *The Good Life*: Richard Briers, Felicity Kendal, Paul Eddington and Penelope Keith

The Evening is Calm with Dame Sybil Thorndyke and Malcolm Hayes

'The experiment in broadcasting from Parliament and coverage of the first Referendum ever held in this country presented a double challenge to BBC Radio in 1975 . . . .'

'There were two interesting developments in community broadcasting. At the end of the year Radio Highland at Inverness started broadcasting to a widely scattered audience of 200,000 people – a quarter of them Gaelic speakers – in the North and West of Scotland and along part of the Moray Firth. Earlier, the BBC mounted a short, closed-circuit experiment in broadcasting from a small-scale local station at Barrow-in-Furness. A team of eight people produced up to three hours' programmes a day . . . .'

'In general, however, the period was one when financial stringency put back developments hoped-for or planned.'

Economy cuts meant a loss of three and a half hours broadcasting a week and the inability to 'split the network' during Test Matches so as to continue providing music for listeners. Nevertheless, the listening figures suggest a slight increase in Radio 3's audiences over the year.

Despite the loss of 45 hours airtime a week in the economy cuts introduced early in 1975, Radios 1 and 2 have continued to attract some of the largest radio audiences in the United Kingdom.

One development has been an increased use of women announcers for both news-reading and general programmes.

Among the innovations on Radio 3 was the first live inter-continental stereo relay, broadcast from Tokyo at the end of the BBC Symphony Orchestra's Japanese tour.

As part of the economies, Radio 4 now broadcasts some programmes simultaneously with Radio 3 during the daytime on Saturday and on Tuesday evening. The initial changes led to some loss of audience and in the autumn Saturday broadcasting on Radio 4 was largely redesigned. One very successful innovation was a programme of popular classical music, presented by Robin Ray.

On the eve of the American Bicentennial celebrations, an American historian, Daniel J. Boorstin, was an appropriate choice as Reith Lecturer.

Down Your Way: Brian Johnston with postmistress Miss Peggy Butler (top); *Weekend* presenters (centre, left) Judith Chalmers and Norman Tozer; *You and Yours*: Molly Price-Owen and John Turtle (left); and (above) *Brain of Britain 1975*: Winifred Lawson

Local Radio

	Medium Wave	Vhf
Birmingham	206	95.6
Blackburn	351	96.4
Brighton	202	95.3
Bristol	194	95.5
Carlisle	206 & 397	95.6
Cleveland	194	96.6
Derby	269	94.2 & 96.5
Humberside	202	96.9
Leeds	271	92.4
Leicester	188	95.1
London	206	94.9
Manchester	206	95.1
Medway	290	96.7
Merseyside	202	95.8
Newcastle	206	95.4
Nottingham	197	95.4
Oxford	202	95.2
Sheffield	290	88.6 & 97.4
Solent	188 & 301	96.1
Stoke-on-Trent	200	96.1

In its evidence to the Annan Committee on the Future of Broadcasting, the BBC stated its firm belief that 'Local Radio will be the main growth area in radio during the last quarter of this century.' Starting in 1967, the pattern so far is 20 BBC stations, reaching 70 per cent of the population in England. Future hopes include a number of smaller stations, offering a local service to communities of less than 100,000.

It is estimated that an eventual total of 65 stations, covering the whole of England, would take about 60p a year at to-day's prices from each licence fee – fractionally more than 1p a week.

JOANNE ABRAHAM
SATURDAY SHOW
MALCOLM JAY
206
BBC RADIO BIRMINGHAM
206 MEDIUM WAVE
NEWSROOM

During the year, Radio 4's *Today* programme, under new editorship, was jointly presented from London & Manchester – where Brian Redhead joined the team (right).

Anne Nightingale's Request Show (far left); *Private Lives* – Saturday night theatre, with Paul Scofield and Patricia Routledge (left); *Malcolm Jay's Saturday Show* – Radio Birmingham (bottom left) and *You Don't Have To Be Jewish* – Radio London, Michael Freedland with Dr. Donald Coggan, the Archbishop of Canterbury and Dr. Immanuel Jakobovits, the Chief Rabbi (below)

Following last year's experiment – in which Political Editor David Holmes
took a leading part – the House of Commons passed a motion on 16 March 1976,
saying 'that this House supports the proposal that public sound
broadcasting of its proceedings should be arranged on a permanent basis'.
A similar motion was passed in the House of Lords.
It is hoped permanent broadcasting will start next year.

The year under review brought a new dimension of urban violence to Britain, says the Annual Report, and with it special problems for BBC News. These highlighted the sometimes conflicting demands which can arise between police requirements and the journalistic responsibility to report to the public as fully as possible. First at a London restaurant, then in a flat, armed men held ordinary members of the public hostage, and listened continuously to the radio in the hope of hearing news of police counter-moves from news bulletins.

'BBC Radio withheld certain information, which it was thought might help the gunmen, even to the extent of holding back news of the release of one hostage at the request of the police.

'This co-operation went a stage further when a girl was kidnapped in London. In an unprecedented move, the BBC and the Press kept totally silent until the girl was found unharmed more than a week later, thus vindicating the voluntary embargo. Any suppression of information, no matter how good the reason, is bound to cause concern to editors, but talks between editors and the appropriate authorities took place to work out procedures which would not only enable the media to carry out their task of keeping the public properly informed but also avoid loss of life . . .

Governor George Wallace interviewed by David Dimbleby in *Panorama* (top);
a familiar scene for BBC reporters and camera crews in Northern Ireland, (above)

News and current affairs:
Lebanon, Rhodesia, Angola, and the Cod War

Lord Montgomery's funeral

External Services

'Evidence,' says the annual report, 'suggests that the BBC has a larger regular audience, worldwide, than any other external broadcaster.

'It indicates, further, that in many areas – in the Arab world, in the Indian sub-continent, in West Africa – the relevant BBC Services have a sufficiently large audience to rank as widely accepted alternatives to the local media and often have a larger following than all their competitors taken together. That is true, for instance, of the Indian sub-continent, where the latest survey of listening to the Urdu Service among urban adults in Pakistan indicates a regular following of 28 per cent, whereas Moscow, Peking and the Voice of America have a following of only two per cent each and Deutsche Welle one per cent . . . .'

Anatol Goldberg, a familiar voice to listeners in Russia (right); and the World Service continuity suite (below)

Scotland

Referring to financial stringency and its effect upon development plans, the National Broadcasting Council for Scotland says that 'the changed economic and political situation of Scotland . . . has demanded more development, more finance and more autonomy for the National Region, not less.

'Increasing understanding of Scotland's unique needs on the part of the central BBC authorities,' says the report, 'augurs well for the future . . . .'

It adds: 'Within financial constraints, Scotland has genuine freedom to devise its own output for Scottish use, and, while the general public often does not realise just how severely these constraints limit this output, this is an important devolutionary liberty. But the Council is concerned that Scotland should secure greater access to network time and money if it is to be seen as part of the UK'.

Play for Today – *Willie Rough*:
James Grant and Joe Brady (top);
This Old House: Jack House with Molly Weir
(above);
The Sounds of Scotland: Rod Stewart
(centre, right);
and *John McNab*: Derek Godfrey, James Maxwell and
Bernard Horsfall (right)

Seven Star Scotch: Andy Stewart and Jimmy Logan

Wales

Referring to the proposal that a fourth
television network should be provided in
Wales for a new service, mainly in the Welsh
language, the National Broadcasting Council
for Wales says in its annual report: 'It is of
course extremely unfortunate and frustrating
that just at the time when there are realistic
agreed plans for the development of radio
and television services to resolve the long-
standing difficulties faced by BBC Wales,
the economic situation in the country as a
whole should be such as to delay the
implementation of these plans'.

It adds: 'Despite the financial problems of the
year under review, there were welcome signs
that the development of BBC Wales was
continuing, albeit at a slower pace than had
been planned.'

The Max Boyce Show (top) and
Y Meistr: Gareth Edwards (above)
from BBC Wales

Northern Ireland

'. . . the main preoccupation during the year – apart from the continuing need to report and fully reflect the troubled situation in the province – was the development of Radio Ulster, doubling the output of local programmes and providing the choice of a fifth BBC radio channel in Northern Ireland. In the past any locally-originated radio programme in Northern Ireland involved the loss to local listeners of a network programme on Radio 4, and with the ever increasing pressure of news and current affairs there was less time in which to reflect the other more encouraging and constructive aspects of life . . . .'

Friday Night is Music Night:
The BBC Northern Ireland Orchestra (top);
Vince Savile with Slade in
Nine Five on Thursday (above)

Play for Today: *The Squad*

England

Come Dancing, from the Birmingham network production centre, which reached its 25th anniversary (top, left);
The World About Us: Dr. David Bellamy on *An Island Called Danger* (top, right); and The Fairey Band, winners
of the North–west Television contest *Champion Brass* (above)

Living on the Land, a network contribution from Manchester (top, left);
Going For a Song, with Arthur Negus, from Bristol (top, right);
25th anniversary of *The Archers*, produced for BBC Radio from Birmingham (above, left);
and *Gardeners' World* with Peter Seabrook and Arthur Billett (above, right) also from Birmingham.

On our patronage of music and the arts we are happy to quote this:

'Long-playing records, paperbacks, our public library service and the Arts Council of Great Britain have all greatly enhanced enjoyment and experience of the arts, but the BBC, partly despite the competition of independent broadcasting and partly because of it, has done us prouder still.'

'*Support for the Arts in England & Wales*,' a Report to the Calouste Gulbenkian Foundation by Lord Redcliffe-Maud.

The BBC Singers with conductor John Poole

Royal Ballet in Battersea Park (top, left);
Menuhin: David Attenborough interviews
Yehudi Menuhin on his 60th birthday (centre);
Bayreuth: BBC 2 special with Wolfgang Wagner,
at the rehearsal of *Die Meistersinger*
(bottom, left); and
Romeo and Juliet: The Bolshoi Ballet (above)

Kizzy: Vanessa Furst (top); and
Play School: Chloe Ashcroft and Fred Harris (above)

John Craven's Newsround (top); and
Rocky O'Rourke: Michael Hills (above)

Changes in Religious Television

The BBC issued the following statement on
12 May 1976:

For many years the BBC and Independent
Television have placed most of their religious
programmes in the period between 6.15 and
7.25 pm on Sunday evening.

After thorough discussion with both
broadcasting authorities the Central
Religious Advisory Committee has made a
number of recommendations for change.
These recommendations have now been
accepted by the BBC and the changes will be
introduced in April 1977.

From that date *Songs of Praise* on BBC1
will start at 6.40 and will finish at 7.15 pm
(ITV will also be transmitting religious
programmes at this time). *Anno Domini* or
future comparable programmes will be shown
at 10.15 pm. Both programmes will be backed
by increased resources and the total amount
of time given to religious television on
Sunday evenings will be slightly increased.

These changes are designed to improve
the placing and the range of religious
programmes. The BBC believes that they will
provide a better service to the viewing public.

The Chester Mystery Plays: (facing page)
with Michael Hordern as God (top, left),
Nina Thomas as Mary (top, right),
and Tom Courtenay as Christ (below).

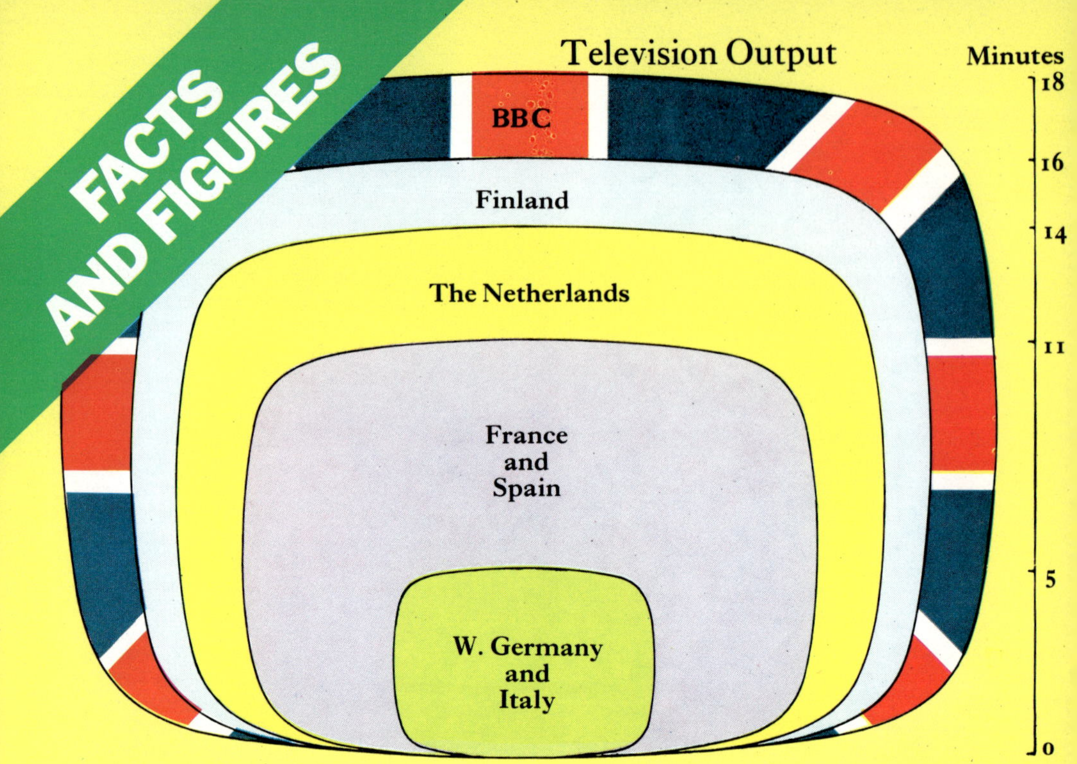

● Britain has the cheapest television licences in Europe (*see page 12*). The £18 colour licence is the equivalent of less than 5p per day; the £8 black-and-white licence works out at a little over 2p per day.

● In each of its 10 major production studios in London, the BBC produces 18 minutes of completed TV programme material every day. This compares with 16 minutes in Finland, 14 minutes in Holland, 11 minutes in Spain and France and five minutes in Germany and Italy.

● In 1975–6 a total of 11,259 hours of television programmes was transmitted by the BBC, including those broadcast regionally. Nearly 1,000 hours of this output was for Open University programmes. *Full details on page 62.*

● Even after charging the use of all staff and equipment, two-thirds of television programmes cost less than £10,000. Only two per cent cost more than £50,000.

● Ninety-six per cent of artists earned less than £2,000 in 1975–6. The highly-paid artist is the exception – only 35 of them out of 54,000 employed earned over £20,000.

● During the same year BBC Radio broadcast 116,555 hours of programmes, including 1,027 hours for the Open University. The 20 BBC Local Radio stations produced 84,539 hours of their own programmes. *Full details on page 63.*

● BBC Enterprises sold 9,000 hours of BBC Television programmes to 80 countries – which means that someone around the world is watching a BBC programme at any time of the day.
Sales realised a gross of some £6 million.

● Best-selling series during the year were *David Copperfield* (sold to 24 countries), *Fall of Eagles* (20 countries), *War and Peace* (14), *The Pallisers* (13), *The Ascent of Man* (11). *Dad's Army* sold to 21 countries and *The Goodies* to 20.

- BBC Publications (who produce *Radio Times* and *The Listener*, special publications for schools and a wide range of books) achieved gross sales of £19 million during the year.

- Merchandising associated with programmes saw a rise in gross revenue of some 40 per cent. Most popular items: toys and games relating to *The Wombles* and *Basil Brush*.

- BBC Records & Tapes grossed 65 per cent more than the previous year, despite a recession in the UK record industry. Sales totalled nearly 450,000, with an extra 100,000 either exported or manufactured overseas on licence.

- During the four-week experiment in radio broadcasting of proceedings in the House of Commons about 450 reports were produced for national networks, regions and local radio stations and there were almost 22 hours of live broadcasting.

- No Government has ever had to write off a BBC deficit in over 50 years.

- During the year the BBC provided more than 3,200 radio and television programmes for schools and nearly half that number again for those interested in further and adult education. The cost was met from licence revenue.

- Most ambitious development in educational broadcasting has been the Adult Literacy Project, a contribution to the national campaign against illiteracy – a TV series and publications for students, a radio series and workbook for volunteer tutors. By the end of 1975, the unit had received 10,000 calls and 50,000 copies of the workbook had been sold.

- In the calendar year 1976, the BBC is providing about 1,100 hours of television and 900 hours of radio in support of the 99 courses or part courses prepared by the Open University. Costs are recovered by the University from the Government.

- By the end of March, 1976, the total number of television licences was 17,787,984. Of these, 8.6 million were colour licences, an increase of over one million on the previous year's figures for colour.

- Upwards of half a million letters a year come to the BBC from viewers and listeners. And that doesn't include responses to invitations broadcast in programmes – they can total as many as 7,000 a day.

- The BBC has 54 advisory bodies. They can be divided into two main groups:

those invited to advise on policy and programme activities in general – led by the General Advisory Council – **and those invited to give more specialised counsel on programmes.**

- Total amount received in response to all regular television appeals (on BBC 1, usually on the third Sunday of each month) was £185,483. The total of all Radio 4's *Week's Good Cause* appeals was £236,834.

The Audience Research Department was founded 40 years ago. It is estimated that they have conducted something like 40 million interviews in that time about viewing and listening. Continuous daily interviews in their present form began in 1939, with 800 a day; now 2,500 are interviewed daily.

- Staff employed on 31 March 1976, totalled 25,963 – a reduction of 117, made up of an increase of 197 in the Regions and a reduction of 314 in London – figures which reflect the end of major expansion in the BBC as a whole and a policy of encouraging regional development.

- **What each service costs**

Television	£million
BBC 1	78
BBC 2	36
Regional services	13
Transmission & distribution	5
	132

Radio	
Radio 1	5
Radio 2	9
Radio 3	11
Radio 4	12
Regional Services	7
Local Radio	6
Transmission & distribution	2
	52

The Grand National (top, right); *Wimbledon*:
Chris Evert, Women's Singles Champion (right);
Pro-Celebrity Golf: Tom Weiskopf, Bing Crosby,
Peter Alliss, Val Doonican, Peter Oosterhuis
(bottom, right), and
Supermind: finalists with presenter
Magnus Magnusson, centre, and winner
Nancy Wilkinson, left (below).

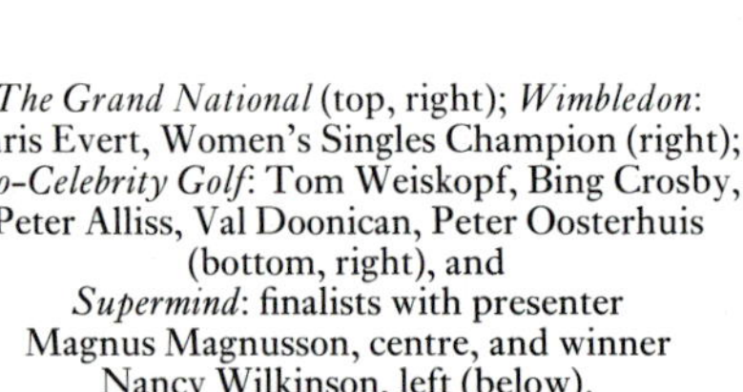

Captain Mark Phillips takes a tumble at *The Badminton Horse Trials* (below)

America's Johnny Miller, winner of this year's British Open,
one of the highlights of BBC Television's golf coverage.

Krakus yano Atalanta

6

John Curry winning his gold medal in the Men's Figure Skating event at the Winter Olympics, extensively covered on BBC 1 (top); and *Match of the Day*, which had an average audience of over 10 million.

Michael Holding, West Indies fast bowler, in action during the 1976 tour.

Sir Michael Swann
Chairman since 1973.

Mark Bonham Carter
Vice-chairman.

Roy Fuller

Tony Morgan

The Board of Governors meet fortnightly under the chairmanship of Sir Michael Swann. Usually, their meetings alternate between Broadcasting House and Television Centre in London. They hold meetings, too, in Scotland, Wales, Northern Ireland and in the English regions. They are, in fact, the members of the British Broadcasting Corporation – which makes them the ultimate source of authority in the BBC. (A fuller description of their work appears on *page 54*).

The Board of Management, consisting of the most senior BBC executives, meet weekly. Their meeting is chaired by the Director-General, Sir Charles Curran, who is the BBC's chief executive and its editor-in-chief – particularly in relation to news and current affairs programmes on radio and television. He and his colleagues are responsible for the running of the BBC – its programmes, its equipment, its money and its staff management – for all of which they're answerable to the Governors.

Other members of the Board of Management, chaired weekly by the Director-General, are:

Sir Huw Wheldon,
Special Adviser to the Director-General;

James Redmond,
Director of Engineering;

Kenneth Lamb,
Director, Public Affairs;

Maurice Tinniswood,
Director of Personnel;

Paul Hughes,
Director of Finance.

Dr. Glyn Tegai Hughes
**National Governor
for Wales.**

Bill O'Hara
**National Governor
for Northern Ireland.**

Prof. Alan Thompson
**National Governor
for Scotland.**

One vacancy

Lord Feather,
former TUC
General Secretary,
died on
28 July 1976.

George Howard

Lord Greenhill of Harrow

Mrs Stella Clarke

Philip Chappell

Director-General
(Chief executive & editor-in-chief)
Sir Charles Curran

Managing Director
Television
Ian Trethowan

Managing Director
Radio
Howard Newby

Managing Director
External Broadcasting
Gerard Mansell

But what do the Governors do?

They're 12 **'trustees for the national interest'** – watchdogs for the viewers and listeners and licence-holders. They're a constitutional buffer against political interference with BBC programmes. They appoint the senior executives – the top 30 or 40, starting with the Director-General – a choice that determines over the years what sort of body the BBC is and what sort of programmes it puts out. They deal, too, with major financial questions.

And in this year's report to Parliament they tell of three of the major issues they tackled – news and current affairs, bad language and television drama.

News & current affairs took up a good deal of their time – a good example, they say, of the Board challenging the assumptions of the professionals about the nature of broadcast journalism. There had been criticism, too, that the BBC had failed to report industrial affairs adequately.

'In one form, the criticisms suggested that we favoured consumers at the expense of producers. In another, that we reflected industry only in its moments of conflict and not in the far more numerous moments when it was operating smoothly. We were accused of showing unions only as disturbers of a peaceful situation and management only as unconsidering profit-seekers exploiting employees and public whenever opportunity presented. We recognised that somewhere between the extremes of the criticisms directed at us there remained a certain truthfulness which perhaps, at its most innocuous, reflected national attitudes towards industry and those who in practice produce the nation's wealth. During the year under review, therefore, we began to explore how we might bring programme-makers into a fresh relationship with the spokesmen of both sides of industry and of consumers.*

*On 18 October 1976, the Governors announced a new Consultative Group on Industrial & Business Affairs.

The BBC doesn't appoint the Board of Governors.

'In two other areas, the Board exercised its trustee role similarly. We were concerned at one time about the extent to which **bad language** was finding its way into programmes where, on any reasonable grounds, it had no place to be. We knew from the correspondence which reached us and from our own observations, as well as from the feelings of some of us as individual members of the public, that bad language can cause a degree of offence to some people which wholly removes their pleasure from listening or viewing. It is, therefore, important that such offence should not be provoked needlessly, despite the greater acceptance by large numbers of people especially many of the young, of bad language as an element in everyday speech. We thought that the time had come to say as much to television and radio producers and so we did. That there is something of a pendulum effect in these matters may be shown by the fact that as we were expressing our views to the two services a senior member of the television service was already issuing an instruction in the same terms.

'We devoted time to considering *Days of Hope*, the quartet of television plays which dealt with a particular interpretation of the General Strike and the decade which preceded it. The bias of the plays was unmistakable and sufficiently strong to encourage Members of Parliament and others to suggest that the plays should not have been broadcast. Denunciations of them as propaganda were heard from several quarters. In considering the criticisms which were felt by members of the Board and expressed to them strongly, we looked at the wide range of plays presented by the BBC. The four plays were only part of an output of several hundred productions each year which ranged from classic serials to *Z Cars* and *Dr. Who*. **Committed or polemical drama** of the kind which they represented ought, we believed, to have a place in such a wide ranging output whether the commitment was to the Left, as in this case, or to the Right as it might be in a future play. The fact that on this occasion the four plays were presented in rapid succession gave them an apparently greater significance at the time than their position within the rest of the output warranted. We would welcome equally work of comparable artistic merit from other parts of the political spectrum.'

The Queen does, on the advice of the Government.

The Soviet author and dissident, Alexander
Solzhenitsyn (above), made a world-wide impact
with his broadcasts, including an interview on
Panorama and a specially-commissioned talk
described by Radio 3's Controller,
Stephen Hearst, as 'a passionately argued
address to Britain and the West'. A subsequent
broadcast led the Soviet authorities to cancel an
invitation to the BBC's Director-General to visit
Leningrad

Tomorrow's World: Raymond Baxter with
Concorde (left); and BBC cameraman
and mountaineer Mick Burke who was killed on
Mount Everest (right)

You've got a *right* to complain.
It's *your* Corporation.
You paid for the licence.
(If you didn't *we'd* complain!)

*If you're not satisfied with the BBC's reply
(and if you think that you or your
organisation have been unjustly or unfairly
treated in a programme) contact:*

Letters about television and radio
programmes should be sent to:

**Head of BBC Programme
Correspondence Section,
Broadcasting House, London W1A 1AA.**

He will see that your opinions and
suggestions are carefully considered –
and referred to the most senior levels of the
BBC if necessary.

Phone calls: ask for Duty Office (the
headquarters no. is: 01-580 4468).

Main points of calls and letters are noted
and circulated to BBC management and
programme-makers.

The BBC Programmes Complaints Commission.
This was set up by the BBC in 1971. But it's
independent. Its members are Sir Edmund
Compton (chairman), Sir Henry Fisher and
Baroness Serota. They deal with complaints
from people or organisations who believe
they've been treated unjustly or unfairly in a
programme; they *don't* deal with general
complaints about the nature or quality of
programmes, though (complain to the
BBC about that). Their adjudications are
published by the BBC; the Commission can
ask for them to be broadcast. Some examples
of issues they have raised with the BBC
following complaints: the unauthorised
quotation of private correspondence;
questions arising from complaints about
consumer programmes; the fictional
characterisation of real-life organisations.
If you think your complaint is one for the
Commission, write to them at:

31 Queen Anne's Gate, London, SW1H 9BU.
Telephone: 01-839 6894.

How to make your own programme

You – or your group or organisation –
can apply for air-time on BBC 2 to
make your own television programme in
the *Open Door* series.

Details and application forms from:

Community Programmes Unit,
BBC Television Centre,
Wood Lane, London W I 2 8QT.

Some BBC regional and local stations are offering a
similar service for issues of local concern.

. . . or join in one of ours

Tickets for radio or television audience shows
are obtainable by writing to:

The BBC Ticket Unit,
Broadcasting House, London W I A 4WW.

Send your letter a month in advance, please,
and send a stamped addressed envelope.
Of course, we can't always guarantee you'll be lucky
for the more popular shows.
Two other points:
normally, there's a limit of one or two double tickets;
and children's ages should always be stated.

That's Life: Kieran Prendiville,
Esther Rantzen and Glyn
Worsnip (left); and
Three Men in a Boat: Tim Curry,
Stephen Moore and Michael
Palin (right)

Top of the Pops:
Mud (below)

60

Hours of output 1975–6

Television	Network programmes			Regional Services Only	Total	
	BBC 1	BBC 2	*Total*		*Total*	
	Hours	*Hours*	*Hours*	*Hours*	*Hours*	%
Programmes produced in London	3,150	1,652	4,802		4,802	42·7
Programmes produced in regions:						
England – Birmingham	316	141	457	196	653	
– Manchester	199	213	412	172	584	
– Bristol	106	83	189	167	356	
– Norwich	2	1	3	170	173	
– Newcastle	4		4	175	179	
– Leeds	6	1	7	170	177	
– Southampton	3		3	178	181	
– Plymouth	4		4	165	169	
Northern Ireland	16	8	24	291	315	
Scotland	87	54	141	397	538	
Wales	88	24	112	697	809	
Total programmes produced in regions	831	525	1,356	2,778	4,134	36·7
	3,981	2,177	6,158	2,778	8,936	
British & foreign feature films & series	843	484	1,327		1,327	11·8
	4,824	2,661	7,485	2,778	10,263	
Open University	33	963	996		996	8·8
Total hours of broadcasting	4,857	3,624	8,481	2,778	11,259	100·0

Programme analysis 1975–6

Television networks	BBC 1		BBC 2		Total	
	Hours	%	*Hours*	%	*Hours*	%
BBC productions						
Current affairs, features & documentaries	841	17·3	781	21·6	1,622	19·1
Sport	641	13·2	408	11·3	1,049	12·4
Children's programmes	594	12·2	123	3·4	717	8·4
Drama	311	6·4	182	5·0	493	5·8
Light entertainment	335	6·9	154	4·2	489	5·8
News	232	4·8	156	4·3	388	4·6
Schools	359	7·4			359	4·2
Further education	210	4·3	109	3·0	319	3·8
Music	28	0·6	116	3·2	144	1·7
Religion	126	2·6	11	0·3	137	1·6
Programmes in Welsh	58	1·2			58	0·7
Continuity	246	5·1	137	3·8	383	4·5
	3,981	82·0	2,177	60·1	6,158	72·6
British & foreign feature films & series	843	17·3	484	13·3	1,327	15·7
	4,824	99·3	2,661	73·4	7,485	88·3
Open University	33	0·7	963	26·6	996	11·7
	4,857	100·0	3,624	100·0	8,481	100·0

Hours of output 1975–6

Radio	Network programmes					Regional Services Only	Local Radio	Total	
	Radio 1	Radio 2	Radio 3	Radio 4	*Total*				
	Hours	*Hours*	*Hours*	*Hours*	*Hours*	*Hours*	*Hours*	*Hours*	*%*
Programmes produced in London	4,356	5,508	4,961	5,670	20,495			20,495	17·6
Programmes produced in regions:									
England – South East						88		88	
– Birmingham		177	152	457	786	106		892	
– Manchester	11	219	379	225	834	106		940	
– Bristol		25	127	382	534	105		639	
– Norwich						546		546	
– Newcastle						106		106	
– Southampton						21		21	
– Plymouth						502		502	
Northern Ireland		51	110	23	184	1,632		1,816	
Scotland		72	197	48	317	2,064		2,381	
Wales		10	173	38	221	2,342		2,563	
Programmes produced in regions	11	554	1,138	1,173	2,876	7,618		10,494	9·0
	4,367	6,062	6,099	6,843	23,371	7,618		30,989	
Local radio							84,539	84,539	72·5
	4,367	6,062	6,099	6,843	23,371	7,618	84,539	115,528	
Open University			754	273	1,027			1,027	0·9
Total hours of broadcasting	4,367	6,062	6,853	7,116	24,398	7,618	84,539	116,555	100·0

Programme analysis 1975–6

Radio networks	Radio 1		Radio 2		Radio 3		Radio 4		Total	
	Hours	*%*	*Hours*	*%*	*Hours*	*%*	*Hours*	*%*	*Hours*	*%*
Music	3,911	89·6	4,580	75·5	4,673	68·2	264	3·7	13,428	55·0
Current affairs, features & documentaries	137	3·1	5	0·1	331	4·8	3,304	46·4	3,777	15·5
News	94	2·2	428	7·1	181	2·7	907	12·8	1,610	6·6
Drama			125	2·1	201	2·9	942	13·2	1,268	5·2
Sport	12	0·3	496	8·2	139	2·0	2		649	2·7
Light entertainment	7	0·2	248	4·1	7	0·1	340	4·8	602	2·5
Religion	27	0·6	104	1·7	40	0·6	267	3·8	438	1·8
Schools							469	6·6	469	1·9
Further education					258	3·8	67	0·9	325	1·3
Children's programmes	177	4·0			41	0·6	89	1·3	307	1·3
Continuity	2		76	1·2	228	3·3	192	2·7	498	2·0
	4,367	100·0	6,062	100·0	6,099	89·0	6,843	96·2	23,371	95·8
Open University					754	11·0	273	3·8	1,027	4·2
	4,367	100·0	6,062	100·0	6,853	100·0	7,116	100·0	24,398	100·0

At the present rate of progress, the plan to bring 625-line colour television to all communities of 1,000 or more should be virtually complete by the end of 1979.

During the year, 51 transmitting stations were brought into service, including the Wrekin main station (opposite), which serves a considerable part of Shropshire and beyond. Cost: about £750,000, shared between the BBC and IBA. Planning started nearly 10 years ago, but work was delayed by objections from local environment groups. Engineers tried to achieve an appearance that blended with local scenery, and won high praise for the result.

Reception Problems?

If you want advice on reception of BBC programmes – or other technical information – please write to:

Engineering Information Department
Broadcasting House
London, WIA IAA

Published by the
British Broadcasting Corporation
35 Marylebone High Street, London WIM 4AA

ISBN 563 17257 6
First published 1976
© BBC 1976

Printed by Jolly & Barber Ltd, Rugby